GRAFFITI FOR HARD HEARTS

Donald Atkinson

Graffiti for Hard Hearts

LITTLEWOOD ARC

Published by Littlewood Arc
The Nanholme Centre, Shaw Wood Road
Todmorden, Lancashire OL14 6DA

© Donald Atkinson 1992
Illustrations © Darren Long 1992

Printed by Arc & Throstle Press
Nanholme Mill, Todmorden, Lancs.
Typeset by Anne Lister Typesetting
Brunswick House, South Street, Halifax

ISBN O 946407 84 3

Acknowledgements are due to:
Ambit, The Guardian, Lines Review,
Other Poetry, Poetry and Audience,
Poetry Matters, Poetry Review,
Prospice, The Rialto, Stand, Spokes, and
Writing Ulster.

'The Fire in the Tree' was awarded First
Prize in the Peterloo Competition in 1988,
and 'The Proper Way to Hold Them' was
awarded Second Prize in the Leek
Festival Competition in 1989.

Cover illustration & frontispiece by
Darren Long.

The publishers acknowledge financial
assistance from Yorkshire and Humberside
Arts Board and North West Arts Board.

CONTENTS

Disposal

Like ladders from the still tarn the fell-side leaned.
With rocks for rungs I scaled it,
at each riser looking down,
feeling the water's skin stretch tighter
over its cool weight,
the warm sky opening wider
at every breathless rest and gazing round;
to collapse at last on a broad and grassy station
slung like a hammock
about half-way.

A fir-tree grew there, and I lay down under it,
its dark bole like a door,
and the sun coming round it through sweeping branches
straight at my eyes.
The fleece of a vanished sheep enfolded the tree's roots,
its sun-curdled wool fingering softly and turning
the broken down-driven lines of the bark.

A few feet away, I came across most of his bones
where the crows had scattered them;
greenish-white and clean, each of his bones;
fresh every detail of his wool,
even to the crusts of abandoned lice
fossilled in the weather's changes.

To be found thus
after whatever death.
To be placed so
in any of life's cycles.
This way cleansed
and no other leavings.

In Dungeon Ghyll

Prickly twist cleft twixt boulders
our eye picks out, your shoulder
white and shy, pit of an arm
half lame. Somewhere the Stickles
out of sight, back of thrust crags.

Here trickle-splash of coy stream
beckons where foot thinks twice,
halting at print of maidenhair
fossilled in umber shade, or drip
of drenched peat's velvet shag.

Each cramped turn of the ghyll
sound of yon' cataract builds.
Trapped between cliffs a moisty air
thrills like blown reed of oboe
or spiralled breath of horns
tongue-trembling the split-voiced
rock home of the river-god.

Wet hand-holds grace the overhang,
buzzards dizzy way-up,
a shuffled traverse round the ledge
and there – sinking like the lark's
wistful abandon of the sky
or hair let down on rumplestilts
from your high-windowed tower –
the waterfall, the waterfall,
the endless waterfall

Still

Frequently remembering
I visualise the field:
two hundred yards of green
with you on the near
edge of it, only half-
in the foreground of my picture,

flesh rose-tanned
to brown of petal-fringes,
eyes fragile-tinted
like the inside of shells,
lips smiling their sharp grace.

Mostly from our pleasure
I recall your hands,
their movement when you gave things,
and your voice
saying especially the word *yes*
to something of mine.

The proper way to hold them

Snowdrop differently spelled – northern perhaps?
Say, *snawdrap:* a blizzard's hangover, the
melting tam o'shanter of white marzipan
yon' cottage wears the morning after,
Dali's flapped dollop of prolapsing time.
Or *snaedroop:* house-name for a Hebridean
taigh' geal, white croft gleaming a baleful
final tooth ayint the glen's black jaw.

But here in Silsoe woods, snowdrop pronounced
pouts like a pebble on the lips, like something
you could suck. And, before bud-break, they are
the slim white teat of winter. Half-open they become
splash of the first wet flakes on window-pane
stone wall or turtle-waxed laurel-leaf; hardly
frozen, little more than milk-white raindrops.

Later, when they've opened full, should you lift
the sepals' pale drooping ballerina
gently as Degas, underneath discloses
frou-frou of scallop'd frills and curls, a triple
inner flower, its petals striped lengthways, like
tiny marrows, or seeds that hamsters feed on.
Sprinkled among this *petit chou,* bright
ochre stamens prick with nips of goosebill.

Their scent is virgin green, of weeds that grew
in Eden, the yeast of faery bread,
or never-to-be-washed cool armpit of
Primavera. Should I take even a few
from your hidden dank shade under the wall
and hurry with you through the coppiced spindle
shy as surprised girls in see-through shifts of
watered sunlight, skirting the celandine,

if I'm to have you home unbruised
I must not clutch you in the hot palm
of my enthusiasm, but rather
wrap you in cool leaves against the pressure
of my hand, and carry you lightly.
That way I'll have you home, your stems swaddled
in Ophelia's weeds: leaves of long purples,
cuckoo-pint and dead men's fingers; where
after long study, I'll try your language; find you new names.

Chrysanths

These then for you:
tough flowers
whose stems are stalks
wiry yet brittle
rather trees than plants
leaves like alarmed acanthus
as if the oak had seen a ghost
and aromatic
as a bunch of herbs.
Rubbed
their scent takes off your head
oily like mint
or eucalyptus
but dry with dusts of sage
wild thyme
and the prickly snuff
of rosemary.
They've come into bloom
reluctantly
holding their petals in
like burned fingers.
I've got them to open
only by looking
so hard at them.
At last
drawn to respond
they've disgorged
gold-mines.
Their spectrum's
sacrificial:
the light's not split
but pressed
till it bleeds suns.
In Japan
they are a badge of lovers
who, rather than divide,
in their embrace
die blinded.

A woman's place, Northamptonshire, dusk.

How could I leave your love, warm velvet-sided valley
full of the sighs of sheep, your lulling slopes
falling away from the feet? The lane slithers downhill,
sallow tapeworm drawn by the slick of wetness there
where the water-meadows smoke with dew.

A car sweeps by, the silk glow of its tail-lights' on-and-off
fathoms the valley floor. Behind me a knuckled elm
draws up its fingersful of snatched threads
into soft fists of blackness.

In the fields, plump sheep like fattened ghosts
huddle their young round amber road-lamps
stood on bales of straw.

Walking and stopping, hearing the pheasants call,
pausing to watch where the rippled flow of a stream
upturns, catching the grey light,
I breathe your mothering air, feel its pull on the heart.

Striding uphill, I cannot keep my back held hard against you.
Every few yards, I turn around
to watch the levelled mainbeam of a car,
free-lancing laser, threading your hollows.

The road eases itself over the smooth back of a contour,
lapsing again to the bed of your waters downstream.
Rain falls lightly on my face and hands.

I stand on the stone bridge and hear it
weightlessly kissing the matt felt skin of the water.
From the rank musk of these warm cow-trodden marges
a fertile mist of the earth's breath exhales and cools.

I walk back,
pass through the gateway of white stones,
unlock the door.
The outside follows me in.

The Cottesloe Nativity: a mime of new love

Like something folded, you said,
like a cloth with folds at the corners
and slowly unfolding.
You said you could see it unfolding.

I remembered only the white cloth
laid on the floor
and the folding.
Long ends to begin,
then the corners turned over,
the sides
and the ends,
the new corners turned in,
folded over and over.

No visible babe –
only herself
down on the floor, kneeling,
her unfolded hands, folding.

The candles come closer
and trembling the hands of the children,
behind them the grown ones attending
Mary enfolding
the unknown unfolding.

Our own love like something with folds,
with folds at the corners,
enfolded and slowly unfolding.

A Good Friday devotion, you driving west

A cross, a man, a candle-flame,
a woman too old to kneel
crouched over her prayer.
While slant light gilds a wooden altar-rail
time wears down stone to silence.

Here the Christ bleeds,
words hide in his wounds.
I quote you quoting Pasternak:
loving can be a heavy cross.
Learning by you, I spread along this pain.

Spring's here. March gales
rattle the saints in their window-frames.
From his spire, the weather-cock follows you west.
By now you're a hundred miles beyond reach.

I imagine your face, as you walk your cold mountains
turning towards me turning towards you at nightfall
like a believer.

Held at arms' length by what comes between us,
on either side, two failed adulterers keep faith.

Graffito for hard hearts: Merseyside 1989

At oiled tide-slack, the hung gloaming,
sea-krill waiting the turn,
came lure of his cruel song on the water,
riffle of girls' feet in the shallows, treading the shore.
From pillow to pier-head, strong wire of his need ferries them,
hearts prepared to come out of themselves on the knife,
fifteen, over and over.

Streets hot as firebrick near the football ground,
a dearth of cars.
Instead, front of each door,
parked garbage piles and sweats;
families picnic in it.
No-one much works.
Out there in the high-rise, between the blocks,
in place of paths or pavements fields of mud,
spread thick with litter now,
like everyone spewed up at once all over them.
Perhaps they did; folk disembowel here.

Not nine years old,
the sixteenth from feeding her father
climbed to her cold bed. She slept but lightly.
Crow of ambitious heart, a heart of stone,
lifted his voice in song:
sweet sound and the smell of marjoram.
At slack of tide she crossed:
snow kissed the svelte skin of the water.
Up the far bank she tore her shift, she ran,
till naked down on her knees at his feet.
And he did to her.
And he did to her
while small and soft the heart came out of itself on the blade.
Warm heart on heart of stone he held it,
till rooted in his skin.
Then hanged her body by the dock road north.

The Wicked move in on the black girl,
Panda Car driver waits.
Yes, we know your brother, we've been introduced.
He's helping us.
My mate with the yellow pullover, he's helped him a lot.
Gave blood in a manner of speaking. Probably give more.
Could I what? Get you a visit? Now that's tricky.
Here, Frank – this tart, it's his sister.
You know, Lenny. The one we stitched.
What say you and me wipe her little pink nose for her?
'Course she won't talk, yer divv'.
Jump in love. We're goin' fer a ride.

Red heart of a girl, heart of this city, heart of my people;
bled by a reptile order of ambitious, ugly men;
I bear for you dumb pain, harsh anguish,
bitter thirst for vengeance.
Ambitious heart, a heart of stone,
there is an hour of gods, it will come to a reckoning.
They shall tread you like gravel in cold clay,
and the earth weep back rubies.

Swash of oiled tide-slack.

A walk-out on the mental wing

Note: Harold belonged to the Creative Writing group at a local hospital.
Lisch aus comes from a song by Beethoven and suggests a candle flame
telling itself to go quietly.

Three hares in the winter wheat today
for Harold leaping:
the hare in the heart stopped dead.
Oh all his life's got loose into the field
and runs with the blooded creatures.
Or else gone up into the flying clouds
to tumble lapwings.
Nothing's here
no sound from the waxen body in its amber box
nought rattles the smug brass handles.

Weep, weep, the scrubbed pink smile of the deaconess
her tearless cheek.
Touch wood the lord's my shepherd not
but out on the bare hills with real sheep.
Away, away with comfort Honor won't stop saying
Harold's gone
the arrow's in his eye.

Then sound the lamentable thump bang shatter
of Shostakovitch Ten, old Brokenheart's dirge.
Let's have some Marxist music for this comrade
mourn him at least with Yiddish tunes from Prague
where he rescued Jews from Nazis.

A lank military Elgar to look at
with dribbled chin and melancholy tash
turned eighty-two our Harold
old gentleman'd the ward during the week
played the organ for them on Sundays.
Forty-six years back who binned him?
Unmention M.I.5.

Always the same greeting:
I say! Don't you think SKEGNESS
an absolutely WONDERFUL place
– better than Clacton?

Over your raised coat-hanger shoulders
I'd follow the back of your hand as you wrote –
relief-map of a boyhood Lincolnshire
its blue-veined wolds and wide unscathed valleys
all the ganglion'd bus routes and the labial town of Louth.

Christmas Eve in the men's ward
(shades of the old workhouse)
as the soul leaves its body in the bed
he left them sleeping.
Walked out in his scarlet night-clothes
let the blithe rain rinse him
shouldered the wind like a soldier.
Then three days' searching found him
worzel'd in a ditch
nicotined chin on chest
his frozen toes
scarpered by rats.

And so the life goes out.
Walks out and out.
It isn't snuffed.

Our six months' sister in the hospital
worn down by itching sores
her heart a turn too tight
in its seal of skin,
came the deft Doctor
strength enough in his thumb
to ease the spring
who gently squeezed the beating breast until she died
sweet auklet.

Through the window, high on a branch,
my mother tells,
while the three of them stood by the bed,
a bird began to sing.
Lisch aus, lisch aus.

Of course it was her soul you fool, of course.
The life goes out at last, and outward always.
Look for it some place else.

Cast off and repeat

By winter fires in war time, mothers not middle-aged
are knitting gloves for us. Flame-light salivates
loose wrinkling skin, back of chapped hands that
dicker as the needles criss and cross. The gloves
mine knits for me have finger-ends left open
for doing-up buttons, shoe-laces, finding tickets.
Slippery crimson tramlines from the fire
slide up and down the thin steel needles as she works.
She has a funny chin, my mother: like a lemon-drop
but rosy. High flushed cheek-bones pull her mouth up
at the sides, give her that I'm-not-tipsy smile.
Her eyes are brown and kind
under the flopped, shoe-shiny tress of dark hair.
Together we're knitting me a pullover
in four-ply soft brown wool, same as her eyes.
She's taught me how: a simple pattern
and the easiest stitch, one plain one purl.
The hard bit's left to her:
a double Vee of orange at the throat,
her fiery love'art garlanding my neck.
We knitted well in those days. Now,
on the blanket edge, fingers pluck at dropped purls
they let slip through their hands in later years,
no second chance.

In the mountains once, at the snow-line,
my daughter found a small bright silver coin.
Seven she was.
Warmed it a while in that frozen lake-land,
then made a solemn gift of it as children will.
I had a locksmith drill a hole and slipped a string through.
Under shirt and pullover it's always at my chest,
cool, like a key for the nose-bleed turned back-to-front.

When she's away,
I fear her fall under every speeding car wheel, or hear
the call of the man-hunt for her in the throaty woods,
till homecoming at suppertime
loops back the unhooked thread.

Mothers and sons, fathers and daughters, still
with purl and plain of love we knit our selves
in one another's flesh. And the stitches burn,
against the foreknown unravelling.

'His word was still: fie foh and fum'

Christmas is coming, the goose is getting fat,
please put a penny in an old man's hat'
fast-forward rattled off our infant son
as gingerbread-hot he jiggled in my hug,
copped hold of my pyjamas with both fists,
trod water, one foot frantic in my flies,
and helter-skelter bob-sleighed down the hours
to his first tear-up of parcels.

Memory beats retreat to another time,
revives soft locomotive rhythms of The Children's Hour
with a man who made rolling-stock talk: *diddly-dumb*
diddly-doom diddly-dumb diddly-doom diddly-thumb –
blood-beat of a Mechanical Mother,
from whose gentle vocables we grew bilingual.

Sev'nteen-eighty-nine, the French Rev-er-LOO-shun!
sang out our sybilline history mistress from her perch,
and forty boys
hurled back the hag-stressed hendecasyllabic.

Rhythms of childhood,
of childing,
of love,
death.
The cup on saucer's epileptic rattle,
tattoo of heel on floor,
gauche agony of his demise, my father.
Or, in the night, rhythm-not-there
though long imagined synchronous with mine:
zusammen, zusammen.

All heart-and-hearth stuff, this poetry lark –

a tachycardiac table-talk of pensioners
in the village of poets?

Intimate rhythms insist there must be more.
Beyond burden of heartbeat, some call
of alt-horns in the wings,
harsh grating music for humanity,
the sound
in Tiananmen Square, in Tiananmen Square
of one man trying,
ineffective, but trying
to put his best words in their best order
and tease a U-turn from a line of tanks.
This stanza-form all poets should attempt, perhaps,
if only once.

But their song was still:
fie foh and fum.
Child Rowland to the white cliffs don't come.

In Search of the Krēen-Akrorē
an anthropological exploration

In this vile terrain
Progress is slow.
It takes each mile of pain
All day to go.

Through the dank rain –
Forest I cleave my track.
Behind me the leaves close
Hiding the way back.

At night trees full of eyes
Gird me with stares.
I cannot tell which of the birds' cries
Are really theirs.

By day these timid spies
Take fright and melt away.
Quite where your tribal village lies
Maps do not say.

I go by the small signs:
A single snapped stalk;
The glyph of faint lines
Left on a tree's bark.

Only today I crept
Well-meaning and too late
Into your empty camp. You slept
And ate

Here last night, then left.
Sensing me near,
Suspecting rape, disease or theft,
You fled in fear.

Therefore with hesitance
Soliciting trust
I hang my tin presents
In your deserted huts.

Will my useful gifts
Tease from your raised fist
An open hand, or release a swift
Spear's thrust?

Simian voices wake
Those azure birds to sing.
You're there. You've come to take
All that I bring.

Alert child, cradled in serpents,
Lips licked by a sting,
How will your Argus eyes interpret
Their own opening?

Friendless,
Apart,
Is your first essay in dependence
About to start?

Return
Strange envoy of the Kreen-Akrore
And unlearn. For the story
Of the pain is endless.

Do not look round.
No footsteps swallow
The trail you lay.
Your heartland's safe from being found.
No-one will follow.

On the edge of town

Temporarily off the leash
the dogs and I this February night
amble past cemetery walls so low
a child could find itself on the wrong side
and spend a wayward hour among these marble tiles,
caught in some freakish game of mah-jongg.

Farther on
a stink of cabbage-leaves
insists how slowly vegetables die,
the dogs nose along ditches,
trespass on sacred Saturday allotments,
cocking a leg to pee on someone's sprouts.

The amber gleam of street-lights falls behind
till furry dark lines the hedge bottoms.
Weightless cold stands in the air like sheets.
The empty fields are sable-soft,
their flesh a greenish musk exposed,
flayed to the stars
that teeter on the brink of atmosphere
mere marsh-lights.

On the way back,
my feet catch in a rip of plastic bags,
maimed polystyrene chunks litter the grass,
the dogs find broken bottles, and the *Sun*
sticky with fish'n chips, smatters the bushes.
Sudden headlights crudely gild
a swathe of hawthorn twigs,
then strip it off, restoring us to gloom.

Indoors again, our winter thoughts are dank.
An idle débris haunts them.

Whale bone man
a Freudian solipsism

I am the split bone
caught in the whale's throat.
When he chokes hardest
I've made my point stick.

Everything he eats
enters lengthy negotiations
to get by me.
Before my arrival
he would swallow anything

like the young man
taken in and half digested
before my time
who not as an exit
but to make him spew
digs with bare hands
holes in this belly
and all but vomited
gripes through these bars
at a brief mouth-hole of sky.

Racked
retched
wrecked:
I am the man
bone
whale.

Orpheus attending
for A. L. Lloyd, collector of folk song

Always between the tracks your singular voice,
recording angel: tremulous, alert,
a low-pitched flute, but syllabled by water-
over-stones, long days in Maramures.
Wrung from a dissonance of grief and laughter,
compounded of all ages and both sex,
a spoken counter-tenor trapped in the throat
of all our mothers, full of milk and song,
its words came gentle as Gielgud on the tongue
but salt with transatlantic, the Celtic vowels
haunted by Appalachian cadences.
Wenceslaus-treading in the steps of Bartok,
ear keened to the earth through the feet,
you taped for the ends of time those wauling cries
that birthed and death'd our ancestors.
Sounds to screw the gut or race the heart-beat.
Work-songs from Eboli, hot dust on the notes,
Balkan kalendi sung for the plain girl
who dies unmarried, her wedding beyond death
to the axed pine, prettied with rosettes,
they plant as an after-lover on her grave
to keep happy her ghost in the cold nights.
To those villagers, song was the soul dreaming.
Or the pained cry of the deed as it flew
from the strings of the heart. A matrix for
journeys, places. Song was society
nor were we out of it. Ritualled by that,
we caught the earth's pulse and measured time
with flinty rocks, birds, snakes, domestic beasts,
and all the choreograph of trees that danced in Ovid.
Proleptic link man, kinder Tiresias, you –
foreseeing the uncommuned dearth we're aimed at –
stored up against a time of desperate new beginnings
all that miraculous circumstance of song
for folk to feed on. Grant when the last bough breaks
your tapes play philomel beyond our earth-crimes.

A posthumous quintet

And might it be, is it now even thinkable
that in the waste of dying or disease
we do not decompose but are composed:
by endless indelicate disjointings
and slacking of the body's silken strings
inside their loosed integument, by what
the sessile bones release into the ground
death is fine-tuning into distant modes,
Frankenstein's monster played back into sound?
Or think as they dissolve the muscles shimmy
to a far-off jazz, like some tired keyboard's
ghosted registration of the worn
piano-roll remotely turning: braille
our blind Beethovens cull from the massed graves.

*

And this: that private parts long waited for,
returned to, dwelt on, purely perceived:
sleight of hands moving, trammel of your gaze,
each known familiar; from being so
precisely loved, might pass over intact
as turns, mordents, appoggiaturas; even
by special grace a melody entire.
Or that the great ones' bodies are grown
developed subjects: Cleopatra's
the composer's own cadenza seldom played;
Mandela's longed-for frame an undiscovered
Bach cantata in the making. And thus,
not the soul but the smile of my Grandam
might aptly inhabit a motet by Byrd.

*

Love's a pre-echo of the loved one dead,
and to be loved makes music before time.
So soon they're loved so soon they're almost heard:
faces constantly visioned, audibly
passing away. For love's death's vampire;
we're made the food of music through his eyes.
And how survive that requiem – do couplings hold?
Or will you surface on the other side
meshed in loose counterpoint with strangers, note-
clusters of your laughter gracing their staves,
while I, drowned in Wagnerian sea-swells,
sing you unminded from some Dutchman's prow;
these eyes transpose you to another's tune
while you're by love re-orchestrating me?

*

No sex in Brahms, Ken Russell says. What rot.
His tunes are full of women. Russell's peeved
that though Brahms' sex is in, cameras want out.
Old scores are fresh with juices, and love's heaven
lies all about us in our orchestras.
Then what far-off surreal event goes on
in Cookham Churchyard – ressuppuration?
And must the worm undo his work, re-cycle
spirits' polyphony to notes of flesh,
or will there be a choice? I hear the girl
from the attendant bank politely ask
how would I like it: in perfect fifths
or as cash-in-hand. And wonder which to count
small change, should we to bodies come again.

*

They're playing *Das Lied von der Erd'* already
to empty stalls. Fell swoop of brass on strings,
Schon winkt der Wein, but no-one lifts his glass.
Lights in the auditorium flicker off,
it's getting dark down there, a smell of gas.
Du aber Mensch, where are you all? Blindly,
through smoke of stirred ashes seeping from
under the hair-cord, shapes are crawling. Thinner
than monkeys they clamber on the tip-up seats.
The maestro from his podium's fading fast,
our orchestra not playing so good now.
There in the half-light, under the chandeliers,
a different band engenders: kissing, howling,
they un-make music into blood and tears.

*

Japanese children at play

Here in the West
our children's faces
are bursting with character
like maps choc-full of mountains
in Wainwright's little books.
Unyieldingly expressive
they seldom leave off saying what they mean.

But in Japan
you can look in a child's face
as a fisherman waits by a pool –
daylong, summersdaylong –
while the drugged bird noons in the tree
and the fish, forgotten,
keep their cool fathom
shadow by shadow.
Time trickles
and nothing happens – zilch.
Sudden a silvering eye blinks waterflash,
twitch of a nose disappears under the bank,
and ripples pan the surface like a smile.
Soon gone –
flicker of eyebrow,
vole to his burrow,
carp to his cold shade.
Only a water-boatman
tickles the painted cloud.

Here in the West
the looks on our faces
come thick and fast
like pulp fiction.
But in Japan
expressions visit the face
after long reflection,
characters lightly brushed on water.

Waiting for the snow

I'm snug in the Wallace again,
impotent among artefacts.
In eight months (imagine me counting)
my head's been as empty of poems
as that dried-out space between
the double glazing. Not a dead fly
even. I sit in the warm bay-
window, finger the spotted cool
slice of this air sandwich, eye-
ball the scene outside. Plane-tree'd
torn wallpaper skies, scrim curtains
of late leaves, hung like tired old
frocks on large-boned fabian ladies.
Something vermilion's caught up there,
snagged on a twig. Featherlite
shred of whose escaped balloon?

On the way down, overnight's
promised snow came as chill rain
in Marylebone. I didn't mind
at all its aunt's wet kiss, let it
dry on my cheek when I got in.
Its damp ghost hung around a while.

The trees lift up their arms. A sigh
escapes. Through the branches back there
Georgian façades announce 'We're here
to re-assure'. Offer their quiet
attentive solids in support
where no-one's home as usual.

Clouds are lighter from lost rain now.
There's a shift in the wind. Colours
are all a bit muted still,
but the greys look promising.

Nature and Art off Baker Street

Daylight moon queens it, thin over Telecom Tower:
Manchester Square garden stays virgin, padlocked,
girded in sharp railings, For Tenants Only.
Ghosts they mean. Did you ever see someone there?
At ease on the kept grass a group perhaps,
not with lutes of course, not mandolins,
but picknicking noisily?
Or on the memorial benches old men
tented in newsprint taking advantage?
Whoever saw at dusk between the plane-trees
hide-and-seek children's faces come loose
from the bark, flit pale blotched lanterns?
Eden's a garden laid to Heritage now.
You can pay to admire it but it's not the same,
the living's gone. Even the pigeons
don't poop there like they used.

Red crane brings down her arm on the Wallace Collection.
Pow!
For the twin carved amphora crowning the outer gates
comes the hour of the Iron Fairy.
Either side each vase, where the curve swells out,
third-degree burns from the air have curdled
the soft stone faces of fourfold sleeping Pan:
goat-bearded, with pipes and grapes, baroque vine-
leaf (deft abstract of a man's doings)
and swept-back user-friendly horns.
It's face-lift time for all four of him now
and away to the masons.
Our Fairy spreads hydraulic feet,
splayed like a tortoise,
sucks hard on tarmac, pays out block and tackle,
three men make fast the straps, one signals lift-off,
differentials grind, and great god Pan
with Janus face, ascends over London
psyched up by filmic Tiepolo-peopled clouds.

Below him in a hundred over-priced saloons
the women's hair is cooking black or gold.
In shoals among the pavements, Porsches nose like sharks.
O Sherlock Holmes look up, look up for clues!

We can't quite rise to that – but are allowed, inside,
apotheosis of a sort. Above the turning stairs
Boucher's coy tarts play centre-fold.
Moist pink inflatables (Smelling of soap?
Involving talcum certainly) all day
they fart kisses at the uniformed attendant
whose heart can't take torture of soft cushions.
His female clone, confronted by horse-
men in quite unanswerable armour,
loses her cool, makes faces; through the strait-
jacket of her skirt, yanks at her skewed underwear.

They're right to feel disturbed. Not everything
that's here can justify the spirit expended on it:
Lancret's glitzy clowns,
those kissable junkies The Greuze Sisters,
hectares of varnished Dutch mud; plus dogs, dead game
and fruit. Better have stuck with dirty Pan.
But there are eyes here redeem a waste of sight.
Eyes like holes in sacking, worn away,
of Reynolds' Strawberry Girl,
that damn her rich abusers.
Or fazed with melancholy – Watteau's Gilles.
The look Velasquez' infants give,
trundling towards us like Daleks on umbrella'd feet –
oh staunch dark velvet of such heavy clothes!

And, in the end, Titus. His father not far off.
We move between them:
the face the father saw, and that of the father, seeing.
Which also the son saw, while being seen.
Here seeing itself seeing.

The lines of vision cross.
Our eyes make one in this dance now,
or best not break Pan's sleep at all.

The fire in the tree
a Trafalgar Day rape in the art gallery

Legs-in-the-air, ash tree by Fragonard,
moon swings in my branches. Yellow sailor
tipsy in the green leaves so what does he do?
He cocks an eye at me.
                              Well? Wasn't I
looking my best? Compared with when Gainsborough
did me? Or Samuel Palmer? Dab-hand
with a soft brush he was allright!
                                        But,
though I do not deny to have been better
done by a Frenchman, I am English at heart.
It's down to background really: harvest moons
low on the horizon, village churches, trees
heavy with apples, a few fat sheep.

So I told the frog moon to piss off.

And now some hooligan has lit this fire in me!
Five feet up was this hole shaped like a cunt
which he chucks his cigarette in and walks off.
Now my womb's alight. I am full of this dry boiling.
Like a lion's got in at my loins and he's eating me there.
Right up inside me the flames tongue, where my flesh packs
                                                    tight,
and they lick all my softnesses sore.
Like in that film where the postman rings twice.
All right you fucking arsonist I screamed,
I may not be Jessica Lange but look here Monsieur le Facteur
where my wound-window has widened and watch what I do
with this ravelled skirt of fire that swirls
round my raw insides. I slip it off and on,
I shake its purled white-violet frills away
and twirl like Marilyn. Up here I'm all Soutine,
like Salome unveil my seared luminous meats.

My branches arabesque the sky. God, how it burns!
I'd catch the cool wet moon to staunch this flux
but he's away.
I'm like a lantern now, cracks open in my side,
my trunk grins vertically and my mouth's
full of a hot laugh that's looking for the brain.
Christ! something's smashed down there.
Bastard, what have you done? All is ash, ash.
I am nerve, I am pain, I'm Joan of Arc, I'm gone.

No fireman came to put me out,
crowds didn't gather to watch.
Only the jerk who'd been there all the time
was peering up the hole where it began,
and as my top came down, ran for his life.

Varieties
a sequence of sonnets

1

Oh in her absence what dull country, this
chalk scut of the Chilterns! No crag or edge,
whose mud's milky and storms are drama-less, just
rotten weather. Land without waterfall or
passion, its rivers are a drag; male the bum
cracks where arid hills hide vestiges
of brittle alder mussed with old man's beard.
Worse: the people don't love it who live here.

Then, one bland occasion, neutral in a crowd,
she's at his side, and without touching
he picks up some sense of her thigh, latent
under her dress, and the landscape, re-
writing itself, womans. Birds quick in the hedge.
The sub-text of the scene translates again.

2

When this tree outside our window thinks it's
time you were home now, it grows vascular,
offers itself to darkness inking up
from the earth crespuscular, through bough, branch
and faint capillary twig to encroach the sky.
The rooks from their nests will show where the crack
is. My role it is the cause! they croak. Neither
wants to play Des, we're both blacked up for this,

and only the birds in the trees can say why
so straight to the limed snares of mistrust
like larks to Eye-ties all our senses fly,
or why to be scald raw in the hot pitch
of hate the strings of our sex should lust.
Not plate or acid knows the art that's etched.

3

You know he's guilty by the way she stands:
that one-piece bathing-costume's a half-truth.
She's held together by it, but sawn through
at the middle, and shaking in both hands
as she butters French bread, pokes at the drift-
wood camp-fire. Their children roll in the surf,
but she turns on a stiff hinge, as fearful
of breaking up by some too sudden shift.

He's off in the kayak – will make his phone-call later.
Way out, the island shimmers like a migraine.
The strait where once he eased his blue canoe
is weeping bitter tears. He'll feel some pain
in bed tonight, faking it to placate her.
And this we do: and this is what we do.

4

Is he a bums or a tits man? her mother
enquired. Come, you must know. Well – like head
or tails: it has to be one or the other.
You've never asked him. Look – when you're in bed,
what does he like you to do? Specially.
Nothing? Everything! Love, can't you just *tell*?
You really have no idea of his preference.
That's very odd. Does he fancy men as well?

But she knew, of course, that what made difference
for him, among the anonymities
of parts, was neither tit or clitoris
nor sudden arsehole winking like heart's ease.
A modern Idiot, Prince Myshkin sex-wise,
what turned him on was faces: lovers' eyes.

5
And there'll be no more pain – in heaven?
It will be all pain. It's where pain's heading.
As I that morning made for the white peaks
gleaming like astral toothache on the blue.
Even the stony river, slipping underfoot
its shallow theme of silk, seemed tears
a god was wiping onto eyes. The cold
as one climbed higher, cut the breath like grief.

And then halfway, rounding an overhang,
came filament of music in the air,
while cobwebbed on the precipice far out
a village clung like samphire. Ice on the rooves
had sky in it and hurt. Clear in the torrent
emerald, jacinth, sard: is you, is you.

An entertainment

Focus of a small crowd on a bombed-site
he stood with feet in folds of sack-cloth.
Those who had first tied his hands
were now binding his ankles
while another counted out coins from a hat.
Soon they began to wind thick ropes
round his legs trunk and shoulders.
When they pulled the sack up to his neck and tightened it
he seemed to mock them, while from the crowd
finger-and-thumb milked a few shillings.
Then they bound him again, this time with heavy chains,
crossed and re-crossed round his bent knees and humped
back. As they pushed in the swords, this way and that,
he laughed them to scorn. Tilting at him from behind,
one knocked him forward, and he fell to the ground
writhing and bucking like a hooked maggot –
but went suddenly still.
At which, the ones who stood round
having paid their price and unwilling to leave it at that
cried More! More! and would not be quieted.
So he gave them the jerk-off they craved –
tension release tension climax release –
arching and squirming the way slugs do salted.
They had to admit he was good,
that he knew human nature. Of course,
it was painful for him, with the swords and that,
not to speak of the rope round his neck
which raised an unsightly sore. But he didn't die:
only got hurt. And for them, his pain's philosophical,
they're alchemised by it, if only to silver. Conjugal now,
no man had dared put them asunder.
Unable to forgo even an instant of his agony,
they watched with him to the end.
When, loosing his last binding,
It is finished now, he said, and let them go.

Eclogue for Dov

Run, looms – unweave this future. See Eclogue IV of Virgil

Stray whiff of hawthorn in the woods today,
uric and perfumed:
smell of our bodies after love, bedded on straw.
Top-masts of spindle mewl against each other in the sky,
petulant breezes flap impudent coat-tails here and there,
then suddenly huff off.
We're over our ankles in bluebells under the trees,
an inland sea.
Unaccountable fluffs of white down everywhere,
infantile feathery mewtings on the cress-green leaves
trying to pass themselves off
among mess-mates of pigeon-shit.
Canada Geese on the pond a floating abstract:
tapering furry soot-bag-turned-inside-out of a neck,
close-barred brown sides,
with blank Euclidian chocks at bill, breast, and hull –
Fernand Leger at prayer. When they turn tail,
lift, with the thrust of paddling, their feathered sterns,
and the sudden luxurious cushion of creamy white
flirts, like a matron's bared thigh, buxomly,
it seems like a courtship display. But isn't. Both do it,
side by side, irrelevantly, to their unbeholding wakes.
Wonderful in Nature all that spare sex.
They seem to use up less of it than we do,
honking and bonking,
look less dried-out by their copulations.
Is it purely because, compared with ours,
they're far less frequent, and containably seasonal?
Should we do it only in Spring?

On the ridge walk, the sun from behind pendulous dark clouds
cast the near hills in a blue-hazed emerald distance,
set off by brush-tips of pale limey aspens catching the light.
A skylark fell slant from her delicate bicycle-bell of a song,
elastic, abandoned, the sound switched off cold like a current,
blithe radio bird.

Discordant voices challenge.
The living language of our time IS URBAN
sang in a modern garden Tippett's Dov,
and hailed its coming.
Age of the Great Car? The canker-bearing clouds?
The rainbow fractured at the poles?
And that miraculous draught of faeces, condoms, herring,
our nets bring up these days off Peterhead?
Oh Dov, poor Dov,
the spirit you announced with so much hope
proves antikrist at last.

Return to what is older, stranger, sweeter, wiser:
companionableness of all that's made
with all that makes itself,
a troth-plight in the weave of the universe,
Mater Materia.
Titian painted its epiphany perhaps.

In the upper air,
at the corners of the world picture,
trees burgeon to a fullness,
their leaves fluttering green putti with urgent mouths.
In the shade of an ilex,
serene,
like a brown rock seated,
clothed in russet,
not Mother and Child merely
but Mother and Man,
huge Aphrodite disarms and re-arms Eros in her arms.

Painting by numbers

Outside, the sun's gone in, Spring's late; but here
in the overstocked corridors of Art
the chandelier's a lit magnolia bush
with eighteen shining buds — a modern light
for Titian to show: Venus disarming Cupid.
Maternité au bord de la mer her second name.

She's had the bow already. It lies
on the ground, a divorced brown lip, or dull
unpatterned snake, the empty quiver painted
flat beside it, like a patch cut out
in appliqué from hills of Airforce blue
far down the shore.

                The offending arrow's next:
he holds it away, their free hands pat-a-cake.
She seems with the other just about to clip
his little old man's wings for him. *Go on,*
he teases, *bet you can't!* His cheeks are flush
with jollyfat. Under his tum, the pert
incipient cock wonders how far it can pee.

Will she ever manage to tame him? *Cupid
thou shalt not muck about with hearts.*
Or he ever get her to smile? Say in the bath,
would she let him push-button her nipples,
sink battleships with her boobs, or even
work his soft big toe inside her lips?

                        *A time
and place for everything* (my mother's phrase).
Here, in the shade of the ilex, calmly
her seriousness rides out his play.
Behind them, the ocean and the sky
are turned contemplative. Now the light
has seen them, things will stay like this.

Out on the estuarial horizon
shimmers the faint pencil of a campanile,
our phallic ghost. In no-man's land, a pine's
dark vertical flowers like a ferny rod.
Nearer, almost at Aphrodite's feet,
matt windless shallows of the tide-pool.

Her ambivalent feet: the one, left out
from under russet skirts that would keep on
coming between; the other hiding its toes.
She sits with huge Picasso thighs wide open
under the red dress. A sensual peace.
In ageing pigments lie down libido.

Keep Greenaway away!

                        Too late —
for what's that horizontal going through
and sloping downward slightly, to the left?
A draughtsman's mark? A smudge, from ignorant
folding of the canvas? It starts just where
a tideless Adriatic meets the shore
and slanting in from the right, it first transects
her elbow, under the silver petrifaction
of the fold in the sleeve; then marks her
breasts with a dark mathematical bruise; cuts
the boy's wrist where he grasps the arrow,
passes between the lips (his laugh transfixed)
slides over the cheek and through the blond curled hair
and comes out where Titian's highlight
catches the bald shoulder of a ruffled wing.
Then on, away, to slip behind the frame.

Running the shadowy sequence in reverse,
it's not quite straight. Or does *she* make it seem so,
turning the shaft aside as it would pierce her
by reason of the sombre reds she wears
and her authority? More mundanely,
is there another painting underneath
and this the leaden not the golden section:
dark ecstasy — or just some human stain
left on her silence?

                Transformation d'art —
a cue for Gautier's worst poems. One runs
the risk. Surely the picture says it best?
All art's translation though: language made over
into other terms; why stop at one shape-shift?
It's *just that crossing over* makes the art —
which sounds like Browning, who did a lot of it.

Description's more than copying, after all:
delineation as an act of love.
Why can't one discipline pay passionate court
to another, wear its colours?
As I with this painting, month by month,
in hope of dialogue; of audience at least.

Not to be part of the scene — dressed up, and posed
as a swineherd, or one of the Watch,
and have a photograph to show my friends:
Me with the Arnolfini-s: Me between two thieves.
A pure Platonic union is the bond I seek,
and not to interfere but to inhere.

I keep on coming back; can't get enough
of this *Venus disarming Cupid*. I've seen
mothers like that sometimes, on holiday.
Under Moel Hebog, by a stream there, the children
playing round her, running wild; till one falls
over, grazes its knee, and two begin to scrap.

Without disturbing herself, without even
looking, she'll reach out an arm and draw
the hurt one to her; will fondle it,
still talking to her friend; dab at the place
with spit on a borrowed handkerchief,
then launch it off again to join the dance.

Even the scrapping scarcely incommodes her.
Tickles disarm the aggrieved one; the aggressor's
sent on errands, found a job to do.
And all the while she's talking to her friend,
smoking perhaps, and unperturbed. Around her
a trustful chaos shapes and unshapes itself.

Sometimes there's just the two of them, as here:
the undepending Mother, and a Child
who roams, comes back, runs off, returns, subsides;
losing itself in self-hood time after time,
slipping the apron-strings; learning to be
alone, but in the presence of the Mother.

Eros, give up your arrow; for dependent Love's
the undoer of schooled Intelligence. You'll as like
poison yourself with it, as other folk.

An adult soul means Child and Mother both.
Better than parent or lover, Art minds me here
to be alone, yet in the presence of the Other.

Not Quite all Smiles

before a woodcarving of the Circumcision of Christ
bearing the monogram of Albrecht Dürer

*By my life, this is my Lady's hand. These be her very C's her U's
and her T's ... And the end; what should that alphabetical position
portend? If I could make that resemble something in me...*

Twelfth Night Act II Sc. 5.

1

And it came to pass, that on the eighth day
These men showed up to circumcise the Child.
Or in my case they didn't. At least, not
Till the whole thing got somehow infected,
By which time, well out of nappies, I'd long
Learned how to hold it, aim with it, put it away,
And be tender of it near sharp instruments.

I woke crying. My mother pulled back the sheet. And lo!
Nestling in flies of winceyette rosebuds,
This huge pink cucumber between my legs
That wasn't me. So, five weeks in hospital:
No antibiotics in those days. I mind
A lumpy yellow ointment they smeared on.
Like piccalilli. And how the nurse's hands burned.

2

When I came six years old, for a birthday treat
They took me to see *Goody Two-Shoes:*
A pantomime, in Birmingham I think.
It had for baddie a weazand, clothed all
In piccalilli yellow like my prick,
By name *The Yellow Dwarf.* He nightmared me.
His finger froze the cockles of my heart.

I had it wrong though. I'd thought the word was *Warf,*
And that he'd suffered a yellowing process
Like myself down there. He was a *Warf*
And had yellowed: every ill inch of him.
Strange child: to have been, in all the welter of
Maimed identity, at that age so switched on
To adjectival past participles.

3
And the all-precocious One: at eight days
Did excess of accidence confuse him,
Or overloaded syntax *I am that*
I am? Was he tempted by elision
to extrapolate too widely from early
And surprising pain, *in the beginning*
The word misheard and in terror named
For a trauma *Kriste eleison?*

When they teased up the tight little foreskin
Was he amazed, or had he seen the scissors
Coming from the ends of time? *Yea a sword*
Shall pierce through your own soul also, Simon
Says. It's a rule. In the beginning was
The wound, they cicatrize in heaven.

4
And here I am, again. Logo'd in lime wood,
Subverted in a corner, bottom left.
But *is* it by Dürer? It's *echt deutsch,*
And yes, sixteenth century. But too
Horizontal, the three tiered ranks of faces
Like a school photo: five women, fourteen males.
He would have piled a tumbled pillow-fight
Of melting jags, thrust planes, the bodies risen
Like whales from breaking pack ice, *ultima Thule.*

Here, the folds of the chiselled drapery hang
Content in their relief, avoiding arguments
With gravity. These protest no terminal
Hollow underneath, and are not shaped by
Mystical light as his. And yet, he signed.

5
This chapel, or synagogue, looks Romanesque
And seems a hospital of sorts: the way
He's crimped all his perspectives in stiff
Vertical louvers, concertina'd like
The pleats of Sister's shirt against my face.
A Gothic church, banged up in corridors.

No need to ask who these are, coming to
The sacrifice oh what what what. You can tell
Which ones are family by resemblances.
Your strict professionals are kitted out.
The rest are there from duty and show pain,
Or guard the pure inflection of the rite.
There's no viewpoint: he understands them all.
It's what you'd get if Chaucer could have carved.

6
Standing-room only. Barges in at the back
Too soon for his appointment this old dad
In Arafat hat, coo-cooing to subdue
Arms full of struggling boy-child next to go.
Ignores the round-cheeked surpliced baldy, humming
A *cantus firmus* behind his teapot smile,
Whose sibling near the front sings from a score
With forehead pouting like a pigeon's breast.

Man and woman in the second row, dispute
The centre stage. It's a war of liturgies:
She's the Wife of Bath with a degree,
Refers to a tome; he waves phylacteries.
Faces of short-assed fellows peer round them, fraught
With multiple anxieties of the small.

7
Come closer to this pain now. Attendant on
The medic, Doctor Luke, (it could be, after all)
Squat over a three-legged stool, with knees apart
As if to crap, sporting some collapsed flour-
Bag of a hat, behaild our loose-lipped pervert,
On his arm a towel, holding in his hand
A trefoil cup to catch the foreskin in. This
Makes his hundredth snip. What does he *do* with them?

Head cocked to one side, corrupt old bird,
Always listening or leering where he shouldn't,
His three chins lolling like a triple gut,
Under the deeps of heavy-lidded eyes
He dreams the infants jouncing on his lap.
These days he'd make a tape, record their cries.

8
He has a brother, took a different route
With deviance. Frigging himself, he enters
Far left: that booted strider with bare knees
Who carries upright in both hands his thyrsus.
A long-nosed exquisite come in from camp,
The outdoor life has drawn him finer than
The other. With the bobbed hair, pointy cap,
The deeply pleated kilt and cloak (Why's that?
Is it fashion, or expressionist for grief?)
He cultivates a style to underline
How lost he is with adults, shouldn't have come.
A worried connoisseur of little boys,
He's never touched them *there*, afraid to hurt.
His lips are pursed against the sight of blood.

9
Why is the Virgin so far right of centre?
If nearer, would she try to intervene?
She seems quite relaxed, her eyes humbly downcast,
And might be praying. But that loose wimple
She's wearing gives her lots of room to smile.
And the two friends with her, who stand behind:
One taps her on the shoulder, the other
Buries her face. Could as well laugh as weep.

Too much fuss about male membership, they think.
If it's shaped right, you're in. Even before Freud
The oversold penis had its funny side
For girls. This though's a giggle goes deeper.
Private jokes with the archangel cut both ways:
Mary knows, like her He'll never use one.

10
Kneeling from a stool and facing left, the surgeon
Tosses back his hood, reveals in profile
Balding pate, hooked nose, and neatly barbered beard.
His face, professionally wise, is lined
With more experience than he'll need today.

He reaches out, the velvet folds fall back,
His right hand gapes the secateurs, the left
With a more delicate deployment of
Fingers, tees up the little cock, clear of those
Well-descended testicles. He holds his breath.
His eyes are focussed on the very tip.
From high in the back row, the baby's aunt
Watching in horror, milks her thumb, contorts
Her mouth in angry sympathy. Christ yells.

11

Is it his father's fault, is he holding him too tight?
One hand grips the infant ribs hard, yes. But look:
The other shapes itself so tender loose, it might be
Stroking or not quite stroking gooseflesh hairs on his wife's
Arm in a draughty bed. The child's only screaming because
They've taken all his clothes off on a sudden.
His limbs tense out like sticks, he goes all of a stiff
Shiver, as though they'd poured iced water over him.
He's a little voodoo baby in a paddy, with skull
Of negroid curls, squashed nose – chip off some dark old block.

And is this Joseph the carpenter, merely?
This long god bearded Nordic sky father
Throned in tall majesty? What face of love
Before Abraham was, carved itself here.

12

And still there's one, and then another one, that's all.
Important, central. So similar they might be brothers.
The balder, bearded one turns away right, can't bear to look:
The other does. Perhaps they're the same – outer and inner man.
The averted one has taken off his hat. His empty hand's
Occupied too, its fingers working with imagined pain.

And the soul mate? Bare headed, curling hair behind the ears,
Not much on top, with deep-set weary eyes, under compassionate lids
and heavy brows, a long straight nose, and sunken lines
Down each side of the meagre lips and dimpled chin: I take *him* personally.
Even the bumps to be read in the bald skull, they're mine, they're mine.
Oh self-tired sadness looking at the babe.
The anxious heart, drawn from its own distress,
Content, almost asleep, with pity.

13

Streams, sequences, rotations: space trans-forms
To language in a trance of hands and eyes
About the child. What Word's implicit in this Sign,
Or what dumb voice calls to what seeing ear?
The Trinity's but grammar acting out
Itself perhaps: *the father loves the son* –
Though Oxymoron adds *and wounds him*. Our
Apprentice cuts render a small Passion.

Worst pain comes first, the death before the life.
Two hands at prayer, the mantis shapes a cross
and mutilates herself. We write our poems.
Words die into thought, tease out again.
Inveterate self-referrer, Universe,
With *D. AD. DA.* reading the deep structure.

Strangers

Semi-detached, I've quit the house tonight,
And though it's time for bonfires, more or less,
I light no fireworks, loose no crimson worm
In the blue touch-paper. We're through with all that.
My last child's laying claim to womanhood;
Is her own sparkler now; holds herself out
Gingerly, the bated heart agog,
To catch the electric whisper in the blood.

Above my head the jewelled night-flights trace
Their vectors in the sky; tropical fish
With blinkers. Navigation lights
Pout on and off, filtering star-plankton;
Sound of those engines ear-muffed, walkmanised.
At a far tangent, rush-hour traffic
Races home down the A6, its distant roar
The pulsing of a metal waterfall.

I walk in half-light, taking a stony track
Laid down for Land Rovers, rutted by tyres.
Either side me, hedgeless fields transpire
A subtle, smoky aura. Miles away
Rockets shoot up from village gardens
Prematurely, starbursting space-invaders,
Or falling short in coin-showers, molten spangles,
Fire-drips. Too soon surely, eve of all hallows.

At first they stood like mirrors in the air –
Trick of perspective, coming down the slope.
Then, as the ground levelled, I saw them clear:
Low to the earth and lying in my path
The two flat Sisters, shapes cut out in water,
Templets or spirit-lakes, and pale with star light.
They'd stopped, as for some assignation on a bridge.
And I could go no further, having met.

Like worn brasses on tombs, they're all outline,
Feature and flesh blurred to a shimmering pool
Of quicksilver, quick-gold; portraiture
Implicit in the silhouette, *the bounding line.*
One, in a Joshua Reynolds flowered hat,
Shakes out a parasol intemperately wet.
Her billowy dress wasps in at the waist, swells
With the sudden broadening of a mere

Round hips and thighs, then narrows at the knees
Before the final both-ways swish of fullness
To the floor, embarrassing the feet.
The other's medieval, and afflicted,
With belted sackcloth, hair close-cropped or shaved.
Slant block of the torso and the arms
Bespeak some burden cradled at her breast.
The skull is small, recessive, rained-upon.

If the water they're expressed in was tears once
The pain's not there. Somewhere deeper perhaps.
All here's as shallow as the merest fact:
Language of surfaces, free of metaphor.
The leafless copse, the stubbled field might well
Be taken for themselves, no more. Except
There's an unheard cry behind all this,
Some kind of wound. Only the bleeding's stopped.

I'm like a soldier stood on sentry-go;
Chill, from that far country, in my bones.
I can't walk on. If I trod through them,
Their shapes would slip like mercury, re-form,
And I'd be guilty somehow. Yet Land Rovers
Have given me precedent and done no harm.
Accommodating such disturbance daily,
The surfaces float up again like the new-drowned.

I ponder their long absence in the dog-days,
That sleeping contour dreaming their return,
Its need for just the right amount of rain
Lest the quick downpour render them obese
Flooding the inscape, or a rampant sun
Attenuate their fragile forms; and by how
Delicate a mathematic hangs
Their apparition here, their beaming down.

Logic of meteors shapes and unshapes us.
We share a chance epiphany, these wraiths
And I, scant will o' the wisps, attendant
On the weather's changes, gravelled in clay.
Time's wheeled seraphim or an earth-mover
Could shatter their frame or mine at a whim.
In poems too perhaps, as in this random meeting,
Ignis fatuus mirrors a foolish fire.

Or can a coldness round the heart suggest
There's more to it than that? *O friendly death
Come quick!* the poet prayed, who counted on
Oblivion for release and no more waking.
These shades that glimmer in my path tonight
Tell of a universe shot through with referred
Pain, stray laughter; awareness going on,
But brokenly, the mind having lost its way.

Absolved at last, I find myself bowing –
A samurai who's making for the door.
Their two shapes hold a while, baleful as eyes
That flicker at the rim; then re-compose
In dull oblong puddles. I should mouth
Psalms, under this sprinkled salt of stars.
Instead, retire stumbling, a permitted Fool;
Try not to turn my back; fail; plod homewards.

Shoot-ups of small birds in flocks from the hill brow,
And the house roof dark, over its warm cradling.
She whom, for her calm sense and her beauty,
Others will soon covet, has lighted the home fire,
And we sit by it in company a while.
Like sparrows flying through the Saxon hall,
Out of the cosmic drift and into it again,
Our souls are fully wakened only once perhaps.

After this life, endless dispersal of consciousness;
Thinner and clearer the orphaned surfaces;
Our voices getting quieter all the time.

After Seeing Things

A storm's impending, and the little boat
With handkerchief sail, scuds under cloud
On a glinting dark sea, colour of bronze.

Boxed serpents in the bilge grow sick as entrails.
For Dublin bound, it's throw them overboard
And watch them swim towards England as they die.

Their writhing shapes illuminate our gospels.
Treatment for snake-bite in the age of Bede?
Leaves of old manuscripts from anywhere

In Ireland. Scrape till the parchment flakes,
Then stir the holy dandruff in the cup
And drink. The swelling soon goes down; you'll live.

At the spent surf's edge, the poet with his dog
Picks up a shell and holds it to his ear:
Ebb-tide of silence eating at the words.

When will the monks begin their nightly singing,
Take his head gently in their hands, and lay
Those white hairs on the pillow till he sleeps,

Dreaming how in his orchard, reaching for
Fruit that hangs like purple eggs of twilight,
Wasp-bitten flesh would tempt him, sticky with wounds?

From Underground shores we take our enforced
Journey, his volume in our hands; reading
And inwardly weeping, so chaste is the song.

In the dry electric trough below the rails,
Felted with lamb's-wool of anaemic soot,
A mutant strain of mice make home-sweet-home.

They're fed by a weary slough of human skin
Falling in grey snow from our faces
Who wait for trains to hurry us away.

When there's poison between poets (and who's
Proof against bites?) pass round his latest book
And see what happens: from every page

Beneficent dust will rub off on their hands,
Gold of his lettering entinct their breath.
Those penned illuminations shrivel snakes.

At the master class in Ambleside

Threadgold we were, spun from her rainbow arm,
our guts made over into butterflies –
las mariposas – while the Angel played.

She came from Venezuela. Water to
foreign waterfall sang in her head; her skies
reflected in our lakes were what she dreamed.

Mountains looked in at the window. Try, he said,
to let the sound you hear behind your eyes
go through the neck and out into your hand.

It fell from her fingers, shot like arrow-fires
through air, and made a lattice in our sense.
Sebastian was not more pierced than we

netted in her electric web, flesh
stung into beholding, all theory.
A mercury of pheromones slid up the strings

then found her face, and homed with Melancholy.

Company

Sam Beckett liked to show them hand in hand,
trudging away from us along a road
as night was falling, at a steady pace
(the man, that is) and the child hurrying;
soundtracked with Schubert or late Beethoven,
slow movement of a string quartet, against
the tread. Barely a memory of feet
in the round-shouldered backs walking away,
the coats that rippled like a heat-mirage.
It's doubtful if we ever saw the boots.

With me, she's always following behind,
not dawdling, but in her own linked world, choosing
a stone. I'm not forbidden to look back
yet draw the line at calling hurry up.
We're on the one mountain, walking the one path;
she'll come, I know she's there, her trust
all in the journeying other, up ahead.
And I'm content to sit, here on this rock.
It seems I'm only waiting for myself –
same difference. When did my soul get loose?

I know the thing by heart, and this is what:
a cock's comb of sharp edge against the sky,
the light behind, and then the green path down,
with somewhere at my back the small soul
following, blithe in its confidence.
Animula: something inside, that lives
by getting out; free now, and coming after.
No state so pure as this can last, says the music
in my throat; a stress of violins.
But I'm not moving from this spot. I'll wait.

DONALD ATKINSON was born in Sheffield in 1931, and was educated there and at Magdalene College, Cambridge. He entered the Church of England as a priest, leaving in 1970. From 1958 until he took very early retirement in 1986, he also worked as a teacher and headmaster in secondary schools. For the last ten years of that career he directed plays with the Broxbourne School Youth Theatre, Hertfordshire. In 1988 he was awarded First Prize in the *Peterloo Poetry Competition*, and Joint First Prize in the *TLS Cheltenham Literature Festival Competition*. His first volume of poetry, *A Sleep of Drowned Fathers*, was published by *Peterloo* in 1989, and won the Aldeburgh Poetry Festival Prize in 1990, for the best first collection of the previous twelve months. Donald Atkinson edits the poetry magazine *SPOKES*.